soft spoken

Logan Decker

BookLeaf Publishing
India | USA | UK

Presentation by *BookLeaf Publishing*

Web: www.bookleafpub.com

E-mail: info@bookleafpub.com

ISBN: 9789363314948

First edition 2024

The Girl of Night

Beautiful
Breathtaking

You stare at the moon and I stare at you, both
beyond beautiful. However, only one will
remain when the sun rises.

Temporary Happiness

Do you enjoy life?
Or do you enjoy distracting yourself?
Do you love someone?
Or are you afraid to be alone?
Are you happy?
Or has faking a smile became a habit?

What makes you happy? Is it a person or a place? Could it be a song or a memory? We cannot rely on others to provide us with happiness. When they leave, that spark of light, the idea of happiness and joy fades away leading you back into the darkness where you don't deserve to be. Find happiness in yourself or even a place, and hold on to that. When you are happy without having to rely on the temporary joys, no one can take that from you.

Passing Time

Time limits us all
But we continue to live
As if life's timeless

Sometimes I glance up at the clouds drifting across the sky, thinking of the days when I wasn't pressed for time and felt free. A time where responsibilities and stress weren't a factor. A time where my biggest concerns were which game to play or show to watch, but now the clouds seem to be drifting faster. Reminding me that little by little time is passing me by. Even as time passes I remain still and free with an empty mind.

New Love

The hardest part is moving on. Moving on from a love that we wanted to last. Though it is not the person you will miss, it's what you had with the person. We are afraid that things will not feel the same with another person, but that's the beauty of it. No love should feel the same. Each love story is wrote differently. With its own feelings of love, safety, and comfort. That feeling can be found in another, so do not hold on to a person and miss your chance at a better love and happier ending.

Memories

5

Moments come in life where our eyes can capture what pictures may not. Pictures capture the moment. Our eyes capture the emotions and memories. We experience the excitement along with the astonishment, the highs and lows.

Feeling of Loneliness

I will be there for you, even when you can't be there for yourself. I won't let you experience the feeling of being alone. The feeling of thinking you don't deserve better. The feeling of being invisible in a crowded room.

Broken Hearts

There are many different types of pain, but the pain of a heartbreak is like no other. It isn't easily healed and drains you mentally. It leaves you asking questions like why me, or why was I not good enough? What makes you think it is your fault? What if they just couldn't appreciate what they had? Pick yourself up and hold your head high, you don't deserve to be looked down on.

Quiet Thoughts

It's quiet
The only voice I hear
Are my own thoughts
Why can't I hear anyone else
Do I just not fit in
Or am I just
That alone

Homemade Love Story

I'll give you the brush
If you hand me a pen
You can paint our future
I'll write how it begins
Stroke by stroke
Chapter by chapter
As long as we're side by side
Nothing else matters

The Story in Your Eyes

I want to find a romance like the movies; a love where I can look into your eyes and see our future. With every blink a different memory, and with every memory a different story.

I'll Listen

Tell me the story of your life. I want to hear every little detail and every moment that made you who you are. Tell me about the time you lost your smile, and all the times you thought you were alone. Keep telling me stories until you get the weight of the world off your chest. No matter how many stories it takes, I'll listen.

Soulmates

I've always been skeptical of the love at first sight concept. How could one look predict my entire future? Could those eyes give me the answers? Would we be able to work through the hard times and still be committed. However, the more I stared into her eyes the more convinced I became. I asked her if she believed in soulmates and she said no, yet I still believed she was mine.

You Matter

If I don't matter, then that's that. I cannot force you to care about me. Most importantly, I don't care to matter, and don't want to matter to someone who doesn't care….

Chosen

I always wondered if I'm good enough and asked how could someone choose me. When it doesn't matter why. What matters is that they did choose me. They chose me even when I didn't think I deserved anyone. When I was alone and at my lowest point, laying in bed overthinking for hours at a time; they chose me.

Passing Time

Sometimes I lay on my back and watch the clouds fade through the sky. I hear the wind blowing through the field and the birds singing; reminding me that time is passing me by and I need to enjoy my life, even the little moments.

I Hate/Love Myself

16

Read Down

I hate myself
I'm just kidding
I love who I am
The way I smile
The way I love
The way I see life
What's not to love

Read Up

The Rivers Flow

I'd follow you
Like a leaf follows the flow of the river
Relentlessly
Through each current
Over every ripple
Until we could reach a place
To call home

A Fresh Start

Where do I belong in this world? That's the question I ask myself as I aimlessly walk down the street. With each step comes a different emotion, with each emotion a different question. The scent of freshly cut grass flows through the air. As the grass is cut to regrow it makes me think that maybe having to start over isn't such a terrible thing. Even if I do feel trapped in life I can always take a step back and start fresh on a new path.

Helping Hand

19

I am no hero
Just a man stuck in this world
Trying to survive

I want to feel like my life made a difference for somebody, do more than just survive. I want to make a difference and help others, even if all they need is my company. They may just need to hear kind words or a hand to help them back on their feet. I am no hero, just a guy who is trying to help others out of the darkness.

A Fools Romance

When's an appropriate time to let go? Do I leave first and only end up hurting you? Do I stay and hold on to the hope that you won't leave me? How do I know what the right decision is? My mind tells me to protect myself and leave, but my heart tells me to protect you and stay. So I'd be a fool to stay and an idiot to leave. The idea of the perfect romance lingers in my mind and I can't help but cling onto that hope. Perhaps I'm just meant for a fools romance.

Soft Spoken

all of your insecurities
whispered into my ear
telling me your fears
all the emotions
the voice is screaming loud
however your words are
soft spoken

www.ingramcontent.com/pod-product-compliance
Lightning Source LLC
LaVergne TN
LVHW050312200726
843509LV00015B/3284